CONTENTS

D0244217

Words appearin[...] [...] [...] like chi[...]
are explained in [...]

THE POLAR REGIONS

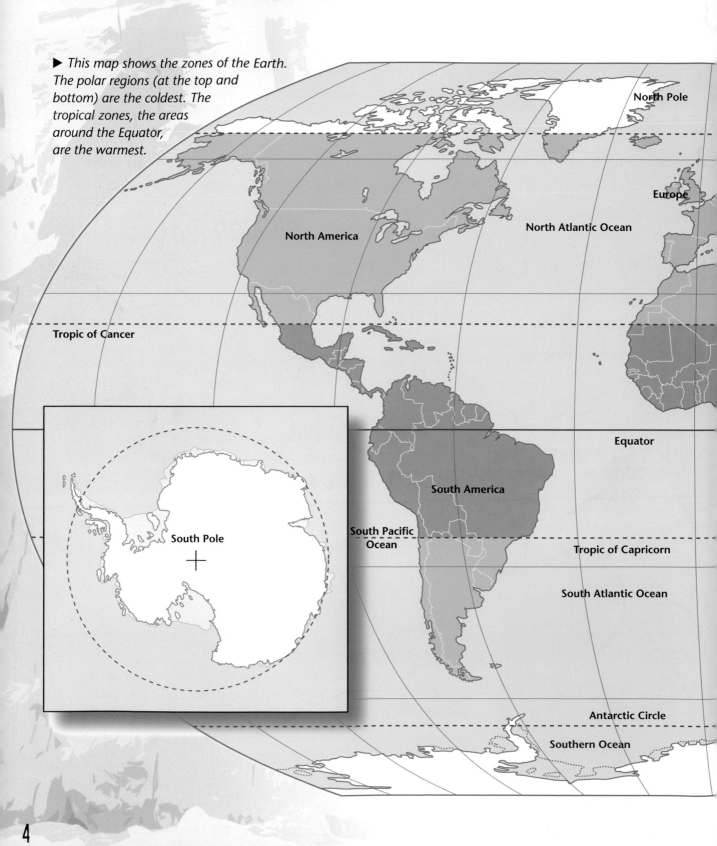

► *This map shows the zones of the Earth. The polar regions (at the top and bottom) are the coldest. The tropical zones, the areas around the Equator, are the warmest.*

North Pole

Europe

North America

North Atlantic Ocean

Tropic of Cancer

South Pole

Equator

South America

South Pacific Ocean

Tropic of Capricorn

South Atlantic Ocean

Antarctic Circle

Southern Ocean

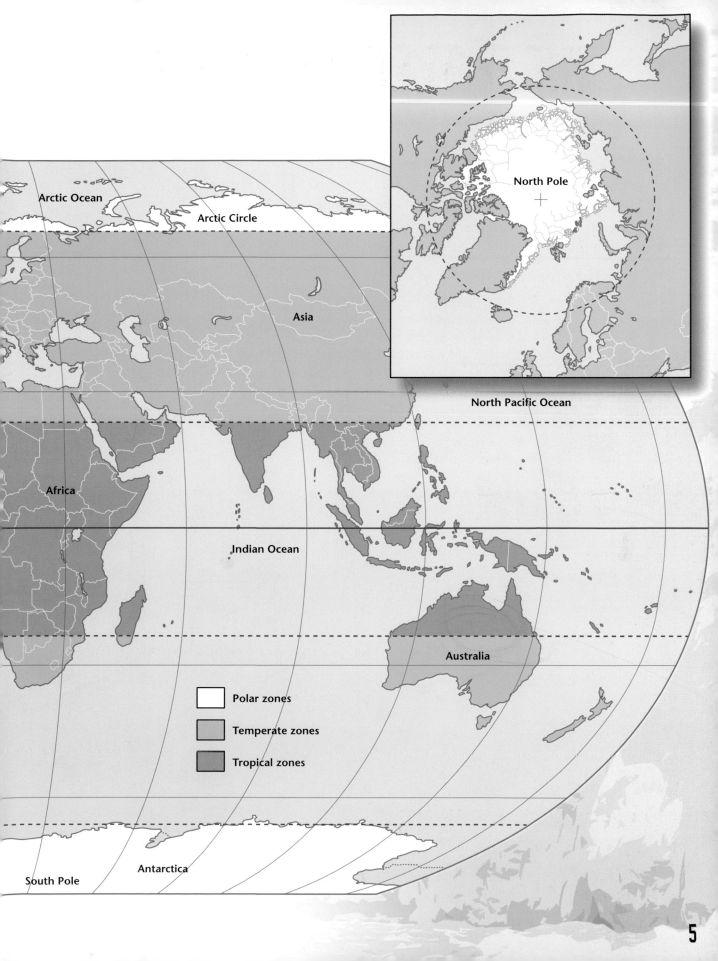

Arctic Ocean

Arctic Circle

Asia

North Pole

North Pacific Ocean

Africa

Indian Ocean

Australia

Polar zones

Temperate zones

Tropical zones

Antarctica

South Pole

WHAT ARE FRONTIERS?

A frontier is the point at which the settled areas of the Earth, or those places where many people live, come to an end. Beyond these frontiers lies **wilderness**, in the form of jungles, deserts, frozen places, and vast seas, that are wild and deserted. These areas are **inhospitable**, or too challenging for most humans to live in. Instead, they may be inhabited only by plants and some animals.

FRONTIER FEATURES

Earth's frontiers share a number of important features. They are usually remote and, until recently, could only be reached after long journeys. The physical characteristics of frontiers – such as dense jungles or empty deserts – can make them difficult to explore. A frontier may be so wild that few people have been able to make detailed maps of the region. This makes **navigation**, or choosing a safe travel route, very difficult. Some frontiers, for example outer space, have no permanent human settlers, although people may visit temporarily. Finally, frontiers are almost certain to be very dangerous to those who venture to them.

▼ *A climber tackles the icy landscape of Antarctica. The spirit of adventure continues to draw people to the frozen frontier.*

The first maps of the Earth showed regions beyond frontiers to be large, empty areas of land and sea. Some people imagined that these places were home to fire-breathing dragons and other monsters. Throughout history, **pioneers**, or explorers of new lands, have attempted to discover what lies beyond the frontiers.

As explorers began to journey into the wilderness, they pushed back the frontiers, creating maps of new lands and writing about what they discovered. Ernest Shackleton, the famous British explorer, knew from an early age that he wanted to be a polar explorer. People continue to venture to the frontier, attempting to make new discoveries about how the Earth, and the animals that live on it, function.

UNTOLD RICHES

Pioneers have also been lured to new lands by the promise of valuable discoveries. Areas of wilderness with rich **minerals** (such as gold or diamonds) have been quickly settled by **prospectors**. The earliest explorers wrote of abundant sea-life, which could be very valuable. They were followed by fishing boats and whaling ships, full of sailors eager to catch some of the riches that lay in the sea. The promise of valuable oil and minerals continues to draw humans to the frozen frontiers.

▲ *Shackleton's boat* Endurance *sinks in the ice of the Weddell Sea. Against the odds, all of the crew survived the adventure.*

FROZEN FRONTIERS

At the top and bottom of the Earth are the North and South Poles. The polar regions are the areas that surround the poles – these are the two great frozen frontiers. In the north, the pole is covered by an area of the Arctic Ocean that is permanently frozen. No land lies beneath the ice. The South Pole is also covered by a sheet of ice, but an area of land lies underneath – the **continent** of Antarctica.

FROZEN WORLDS

The polar regions contain almost all the Earth's fresh water, but most of this is frozen solid. This makes the frozen frontiers unlike any other place on the planet. They are hard to get to, and travel is difficult and dangerous. In summer, icebreaker ships can cut channels through the sea ice. In winter, once the sea has frozen solid, frontier travellers must cross the ice.

▼ *The icebreaker ship* Arctic Explorer, *in the polar sea off the coast of Lapland.*

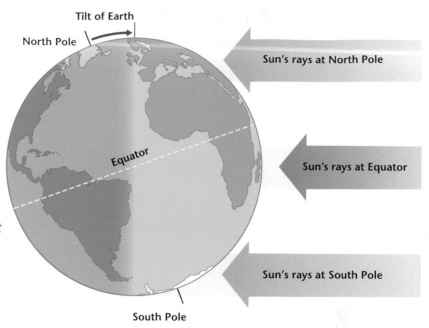

▶ *The Earth's axis is tilted at an angle to the sun.*

When the Arctic is tilted away from the sun it is winter at the North Pole and summer at the South Pole.

It is permanently dark in winter and the sun can shine all day at the height of summer.

Tilt of Earth

North Pole

Sun's rays at North Pole

Equator

Sun's rays at Equator

Sun's rays at South Pole

South Pole

WINTER AND SUMMER

Both polar regions are cold, inhospitable places, where the winters are long and dark, and temperatures fall far below freezing. In the Arctic, the average winter temperature is –34°C (–29°F) and in the Antarctic it is even colder. The coldest place in the Antarctic is Plateau Station, where temperatures can fall to –70°C (–94°F). Temperatures in both regions rise in the summer, but in the Antarctic it remains too cold for ice on the land to melt.

When it is summer at the North Pole, it is winter at the South Pole. In regions near the poles, during the summer the sun does not set for several months. It stays in the sky for 24 hours, even at midnight. This is called **midnight sun**. In winter it is permanently dark, or **polar night**. This happens because of the tilt of the Earth – in winter, the frozen frontier is tilting away from the sun and in the summer, it tilts towards the sun. As you move further away from the poles, the periods of light and dark reduce.

In their own words ...

"With only about four hours of 'night' we have to black out our rooms with blinds and curtains. Some people have trouble sleeping down here, but most people don't. Some people find it easier to sleep in the field huts, where there is no heating during the night. "
Joan Russell of the Australian Antarctic Division on the midnight sun.

ICED UP

Both polar frontiers contain regions that are permanently frozen. There are two types of ice – land ice, which is frozen fresh water that covers the land, and sea ice, which forms when the ocean freezes.

The heart of the Arctic frontier is the Arctic Ocean, parts of which are covered all year round by sea ice. This forms when the ocean water freezes into **pancake ice**, or thin slabs that form at the surface and move around in the sea swell. In winter, as temperatures drop, the ice thickens to become **pack ice**. In the coldest parts of the polar regions, the pack ice is very thick. The Arctic ice sheet is an area of thick, solid ice that covers the North Pole.

The ice that covers some of the lands on the edge of the Arctic Ocean is formed by fallen snow that has been crushed and compacted on the ground. Even in summer, temperatures in parts of the polar frontier are below 0°C (32°F). This means that frost and snow crystals do not melt, but build up and compress year by year. This creates permanent sheets of ice called **glaciers** that cover the land.

▼ An excursion boat ventures close to a glacier in Paradise Bay, Antarctica.

In the Antarctic, the solid ice cap covers most of the land underneath it. There is actually very little snowfall in Antarctica. However, as in Arctic regions, as new snow falls, it does not melt but becomes compacted into a new layer of ice. These layers are now 3 kilometres (km) (2 miles) deep in some parts.

COLD DESERTS

The frozen regions are like cold deserts. This is because strong, cold winds suck away the moisture from the air, so there is little rain or snow. Parts of Antarctica are among the driest places on Earth. Away from the coast, some areas have less than 5 centimetres (cm) (2 inches [in]) of snowfall each year. There is plenty of fresh water on the ground, but it is in the form of snow and ice, and this has built up very slowly over millions of years.

▼ Icy sea off the coast of the Antarctic Peninsula. The ice that covers the land in the distance is made of fresh water in the form of fallen, compacted snow.

WHO'S WHO

Douglas Mawson

Sir Douglas Mawson (1882–1958) was an Australian Antarctic explorer. In 1911, he led a three-year expedition in which several members died. Mawson fell through a **crevasse**, but was saved because his sled remained on the ice above and he managed to haul himself out. In spite of these tragedies, the Australasian Antarctic Expedition explored large areas of the Antarctic coast, and made many discoveries about its landscape and wildlife.

POLAR SEAS

The Arctic Ocean is the area of water that covers and surrounds the North Pole. It is the smallest of the Earth's five oceans. A number of countries have territories in the Arctic region. In winter, as it gets colder, the area of permanently frozen Arctic sea water spreads outwards. Pack ice covers almost the entire Arctic Ocean. Many of the coastal areas of land and islands in the Arctic region, for example parts of northern Canada and Alaska, are met by frozen seas.

FORBIDDING SEA

Antarctica is surrounded by the Antarctic or Southern Ocean. This area of sea has some of the largest waves, strongest winds, and most powerful currents on Earth. Sailing in these waters is extremely dangerous at any time of the year. Here too, pack ice spreads outwards from the permanent ice cap in winter as the Southern Ocean freezes. At the height of winter, the sea ice surrounding Antarctica more than doubles the size of the frozen frontier. At the start of the warmer summer months, the pack ice begins to melt, breaking up into **ice floes**. Seals and other animals rest and feed on the platforms of ice.

At the edge of land-based glaciers in the polar regions, the freshwater ice breaks off in chunks and is carried out to sea as **icebergs**. Most of an iceberg is hidden underwater, and unless trapped in frozen winter seas, icebergs are always on the move.

▼ *These maps of Antarctica and the Arctic show the polar ice caps – the regions that are frozen all year round – and the furthest points to which frozen sea water extends in winter.*

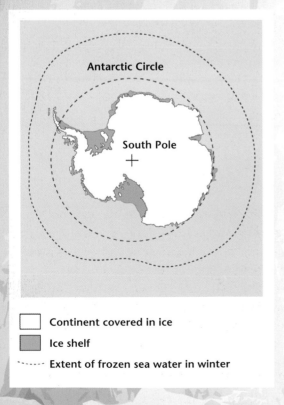

Antarctic Circle

South Pole

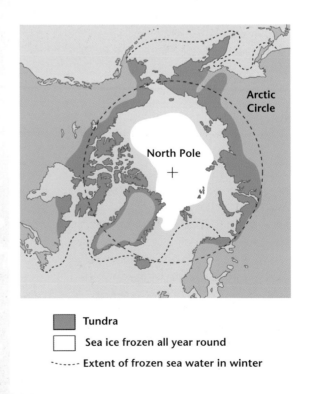

Arctic Circle

North Pole

☐ Continent covered in ice

▨ Ice shelf

------ Extent of frozen sea water in winter

▨ Tundra

☐ Sea ice frozen all year round

------ Extent of frozen sea water in winter

ICEBREAKERS

Early explorers sailed to the frozen regions in wooden ships. These sometimes became trapped and crushed by pack ice. Today, very powerful icebreaker ships (pictured on page 8) are used to sail in the waters of the frozen frontiers. They have a specially shaped front, or bow, and heavily strengthened body, or hull. Massive engines drive the ship forward and upward so that the bow is driven on to the top of the ice. The weight of the ship then smashes down through it, making a narrow channel through the ice. These ships patrol the frozen regions, clearing routes for other ships to use. They are sometimes needed in rescue missions if vessels find themselves trapped on the frozen frontier.

▲ *The strange beauty of the frozen frontier – icebergs float in polar waters near Twillingate in Newfoundland, Canada.*

GIANT 'BERGS

An iceberg that floated off the coast of Antarctica in 1992 made the one that sank the *Titanic* look like an ice cube. This frozen monster was 39 km (24 miles) wide and 77 km (48 miles) long. "They can cut through a steel ship like you would cut into a stick of butter with a knife," said an analyst at the U.S. National Ice Center.

POLES APART

Antarctica is about 1.5 times the size of the United States. It contains 90 percent of the world's ice. The land is buried under ice sheets – only about 1 percent is ice-free, and this is on the coast and steep mountain slopes. The ice sheet that covers the land is very deep in parts and averages more than 2 km (1.2 miles) in thickness. The average height of Antarctica above sea level is 2.3 km (1.4 miles). However, if all the ice was removed, this figure would fall to below 500 metres (m) (0.3 miles).

ABOVE THE ANTARCTIC ICE

Between eastern and western Antarctica runs the Transantarctic Mountain range. This is 3,500 km (2,175 miles) wide and is made up of several ranges of mountains. The highest peak is the Vinson Massif, at 4,897 m (16,066 feet [ft]). Only the tallest mountains are visible above the ice. Nearly all of Antarctica's valleys are filled with huge glaciers, which carry ice towards the sea.

WHO'S WHO

Frontier women

The 2003 conference on "Women's Roles in Polar Regions" celebrated the achievements of women in the Earth's frozen places. Participants included Edith Ronne, who became the first woman to spend a winter in Antarctica in 1947, elderly Inuit women, and a 13-year-old girl who had visited both poles. In 1969, an all-female research team explored the Dry Valleys. In February 2001, Ann Bancroft and Liv Arnesen completed the first crossing of Antarctica by women explorers. As a 12-year-old child, Bancroft dreamed of trekking in Antarctica while reading about the famous polar explorer Ernest Shackleton.

▼ *Dunes in the Dry Valleys of the Transantarctic Mountains. It may look like a desert, but temperatures here can drop to around –25°C (–13°F).*

UNEARTHLY LAND

Antarctica is one of the driest regions on the planet. In most areas, only a few centimetres (less than 2 inches) of snow falls each year. Hidden in the Transantarctic Mountains are the Dry Valleys. There has been no snow or rain in this part of the continent for hundreds of years. It is like no other place on Earth. In fact, it is so dry that scientists have chosen it as a location for testing equipment that may be used on space missions to the planet Mars, because the conditions there are similar.

LIFE IN THE FROZEN SOUTH

In spite of being so cold, dry, and windy, some plants still manage to survive in Antarctica. There are two types of flowering plant and a wide variety of **lichens** and mosses. Whales, dolphins, porpoises, and seals are the only **mammals** that live naturally in Antarctica, although there are several types of bird, including penguins. The only people are a few thousand men and women who work at scientific **research stations**, which are mainly on the coast. All creatures that live on the southern frontier must survive the bitter cold and the long periods in mid-winter when there is very little sun.

▲ *The blue whale is the largest creature in the Southern Ocean. They can grow to more than 30 m (98 ft) long.*

THE ARCTIC

Most of the area of the Arctic is covered by the Arctic Ocean. The United States, Canada, Norway, Sweden, Finland, Russia, and Greenland all have northern regions that lie in the Arctic Circle. There are also several groups of islands in the region. The lands in the southern part of this polar region are known as the sub-Arctic.

ARCTIC LIFE

Walrus, whales, and seals live in Arctic waters. The only animal that can live on the Arctic pack ice is the polar bear. Further south, the region is home to **caribou**, wolves, Arctic hares, and foxes. There are many plants, but these mostly grow during the summer months in the sub-Arctic.

LIGHT SHOW

The northern lights, *Aurora borealis*, and the southern lights, *Aurora australis*, are streams of light high in the sky. They appear at night in polar regions during certain times of the year. They are created by electrical storms at the edge of the Earth's atmosphere. The Inuit people believed that the lights were torches carried by spirits as they travelled through the night sky.

▼ *The spectacular* Aurora borealis *lights up the northern sky. These amazing "light shows" are caused by electrical storms in the atmosphere.*

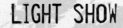

▲ *Mountains and a frozen fjord in the Arctic winter sun, Norway.*

POLAR NATIVES

No humans live on the ice cap at the North Pole, but some groups of people have lived in Arctic lands surrounding the ice cap for thousands of years. These include the Inuit people of Canada, Alaska, and Greenland, as well as the Nenet people of Siberia, and Saami in parts of northern Europe. Many of the descendants of these people continue to live in the Arctic, mostly in permanent houses in large frontier towns. Some non-native people have settled in the Arctic, where they work on oil rigs, and in forestry and fishing jobs.

SEARCH AND RESCUE!

In March 2004, 12 Russian scientists were rescued from icy Arctic waters. They had been working at a research station that had been built on a floating ice shelf. The ice beneath the station started to crack and then rose up in a massive wall, crushing the station, equipment, and supplies beneath it. Four of the six station buildings disappeared. The scientists were lucky to survive in the buildings that remained, with food to last only a few days. The rescue operation showed the extreme difficulties of search and rescue on the frozen frontier.

Finding the scientists was a problem in the remote region. The time of year meant that the rescuers had only a few hours of gloomy daylight in which to work. The ice was too thin for aircraft to land, so the survivors were lifted to safety by two helicopters.

THE SUB-ARCTIC

The sub-Arctic lies to the south of the Arctic, on the edge of the frozen frontier. It is made up of two regions, the **tundra**, which means "treeless lands", and **taiga**, which is covered by forests of pine and fir trees. Like the Arctic lands to the north, the sub-Arctic is very cold in the winter but it is not covered by a thick ice sheet, and it has warm summers.

In the sub-Arctic, the top layer of soil is frozen only during winter. At the start of summer, the ground thaws and hundreds of species of plants such as mosses, lichens, and grasses begin to grow. Many birds and animals **migrate**, or travel, to the region for the food that is available during the short growing season for plants.

▲ In the taiga forests of Finland, trees are covered in snow in mid-winter. In spring, the snow melts and flowering plants begin to grow.

WHO'S WHO

Robert McClure
Robert McClure (1807–73) was a British explorer and the first person to find a route through the Arctic, linking the Atlantic and Pacific Oceans. His ship became stuck in ice for two years and was abandoned. McClure's team had to walk for many kilometres across the frozen sea ice to a rescue vessel, before completing their journey in 1854.

SNOW BLINDNESS

One of the dangers on the frozen frontier is snow blindness. This is a painful temporary blindness caused by the reflection of the sun's rays from the ice. People of the Arctic made goggles from leather or wood to shield their eyes, and these were also used by early explorers. This is an early example of European explorers using lifestyles of native people to help them survive on the frozen frontier.

TRADITIONAL LIFE IN THE COLD

The people of the Arctic and sub-Arctic developed lifestyles that allowed them to survive on the frozen frontier. They were not able to grow crops, so in the past they travelled across the frozen land and sea to hunt animals for food. The Inuit lived permanently on the tundra. They travelled across the ice on husky-pulled sleds and moved through icy waters to hunt seals in **kayaks**. These are like canoes, but are perfectly designed for the frozen climate, as they are almost completely enclosed.

▼ *Inuit hunters in Alaska use modern methods of transport, such as the snowmobiles in the background of this picture, and traditional boats called* umiaks.

Further south, in northern parts of Finland, Norway, Russia, and Sweden, the Saami kept reindeer, or caribou, which they used to pull sleds across the snow. These people used to move north in summer so that their herds of caribou could feed on the plants of the sub-Arctic. In winter, they returned south to warmer parts.

PROBLEMS WITH EXPLORING THE FROZEN FRONTIERS

Frontiers are inhospitable places, where life can be difficult for humans and animals. One of the main problems on the polar frontier is the harsh climate. The Arctic and Antarctic are extremely cold places. Severe weather conditions are a feature of both areas. The ferocious winds during winter storms can make it seem even colder, and it can be difficult and dangerous to move around. Heavy snow is sometimes a problem during the Arctic winter and both frontiers become an icy wilderness for most of the year.

▼ *A human hand showing the damage that can be caused by frostbite.*

HUMAN SURVIVAL

Humans have no natural physical protection from the most extreme cold of the polar frontier. Exposed human skin will freeze very quickly. Parts of the body that are most exposed to the cold, for example, the toes, fingers, ears, and nose, can suffer **frostbite**. In this condition, the tissue beneath the surface of the skin, and the skin itself, is damaged or destroyed. The affected parts first turn reddish-blue and look swollen. After a while, the areas will become white and hard. **Hypothermia**, a condition where the temperature of the body drops dangerously low, is also a problem.

Humans have survived the polar cold in the past by wearing clothes made from the fur and skins of animals. The scientists who work in Antarctic research stations today wear layers of warm, waterproof, and windproof clothing, which help to trap body heat. They also receive special survival training that prepares them for the most extreme cold weather.

▶ *Extreme Cold Weather (ECW) gear worn by scientists in Antarctica. The clothing includes a fur-lined hood, windproof jacket, and goggles to protect the eyes from the glare of the sun on the snow.*

WILD WIND AND WHITE-OUTS

The violent winter storms on the frozen frontiers can drive winds of up to 200 kilometres per hour (kmh) (over 100 miles per hour [mph]) in the Antarctic. These winds are so strong that they can make moving in a straight line almost impossible. Clouds of snow whipped up by the wind make it difficult to see. There are many dangers in these "white-outs" – getting lost in the frontier wilderness or walking into a hidden crevasse would be all too easy.

Sheltering from these storms is the only way to survive on the frontier. The Inuit people in the north build **iglus** from blocks of snow, to provide overnight or emergency shelter during hunting trips. Special tents can withstand very strong winds and are used by scientists in Antarctica. They also learn how to build iglus during survival training.

In their own words ...

"The coldest conditions I have worked in are about –38°C (–36°F), with the **windchill** making it about 20°C (36°F) colder. This was in the middle of winter on the coast. It hurts to breathe, and your fingers, toes, and nose are very numb. When digging out equipment after a white-out, you sweat, but as soon as you stop you get *very* cold. "

Barbara Wienecke, Antarctic Seabird Ecologist, Australian Antarctic Division

FRONTIER TRAVEL

The polar regions have always been difficult places in which to travel. The snow and ice require special land vehicles. At sea, icebergs are very dangerous to ships on the frontier – a huge iceberg sank the *Titanic* in 1912. Modern ships contain equipment that tracks the shape, size, and movement of icebergs. Some scientists believe that changes in climate are causing more icebergs to break off the ice shelf in polar regions.

MOVING ON ICE

Skidoos or snowmobiles, with skis at the front and caterpillar tracks at the rear that grip snow and ice, provide a speedy method of travel. Some of the scientists who work in the Antarctic use special over-snow vehicles, with powerful engines that drive rubber tracks.

However, some of the people who live on the northern polar frontier continue to use traditional dog sleds on the ice highway. "Machines break down; dogs will always get you back," say some Inuit hunters. More importantly, dogs can sometimes detect hidden crevasses, and will stop before they tumble down through the loose snow cover.

▼ *Snow trucks with skis and tracks are a safe way of travelling over the frontier ice.*

In their own words ...

" When scientists first arrive ... they must take various types of survival training. Scientists are most commonly trained on using portable radios, snowmobiles, and snocat machines; helicopter passenger safety; driving safely across the sea ice that covers much of the area. "
Diane Edwards, U.S. Antarctic researcher

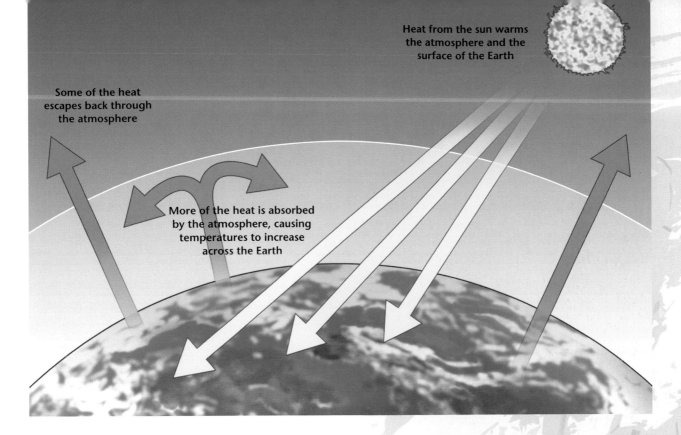

Heat from the sun warms the atmosphere and the surface of the Earth

Some of the heat escapes back through the atmosphere

More of the heat is absorbed by the atmosphere, causing temperatures to increase across the Earth

▲ Global warming is the effect where too much heat from the sun becomes trapped in the atmosphere. This results in increasing temperatures on Earth.

GLOBAL WARMING

It is getting warmer in the Earth's frozen places. Temperature rises have caused some parts of the polar ice caps to melt, resulting in sea-level rises. Many scientists are worried about the amount of **greenhouse gases** that are being produced. These gases trap heat in the atmosphere, and are increasing average temperatures across all parts of the Earth. This climate change is known as global warming.

A few scientists and experts have said that global warming has had very little effect on the ice caps. They argue that factors other than global warming have caused temperatures to rise. However, most believe that global warming will cause the polar ice caps to collapse. They predict that rising sea levels could bring flooding to coastal areas around the world.

FACING UP TO THE PROBLEM?

In 1997, 38 nations signed the Kyoto Agreement – a plan to cut greenhouse gases. However, some of the world's most powerful countries, including the United States and Australia, have so far refused to join the agreement.

It is fairly clear that the frozen frontier is changing as the ice continues to melt. Arctic sea ice has thinned by about 40 percent in the past 25 years. Whether this is caused by global warming or other factors, it has serious effects for the plants, animals, and humans that live on the frozen frontier. How much sea levels will rise by, and whether this will bring flooding and other problems elsewhere, we cannot be certain.

ANIMAL LIFE ON THE FRONTIER

Animals of the polar frontier live in conditions that would be too extreme for most humans. They must be able to keep warm during the cold winter and find food, even when it is scarce. Most frontier animals have **adapted** to the conditions – they have developed special physical features that help them to survive.

ANTARCTIC EMPERORS

Male emperor penguins live in the Antarctic all year round. After the female lays her egg, the male must keep it warm during the winter. For about four months, groups of males huddle together for warmth. The egg cannot survive on the ice, so the male rests it on his feet. A large fold of skin hangs down over the egg to keep it warm.

ANIMAL ADAPTATION

Animals have developed thick water- and wind-proof fur or, in the case of whales and seals, layers of blubber that keep in body heat. They have also adapted to the cold by their behaviour. Emperor penguins, for example, remain deep on the frontier to breed during the Antarctic winter, huddled together in tight groups. This keeps warmth in and provides shelter from the howling winds.

▲ Emperor penguins can travel over ice and through water. They are able to stay under water for many minutes at a time.

LAND ANIMALS

Penguins and seals visit areas around the coast of Antarctica, but it is too cold for large land-based mammals to live there all year round. The Arctic is less cold and, unlike Antarctica, it is possible to move over the surrounding land, heading to warmer regions in the south to escape from the severe winter weather.

THE WHITE BEAR

Polar bears live in the Arctic all year round. A heavy covering of fur and a thick layer of body fat keep them warm. In the coldest months, female bears dig dens in which they have their cubs and spend the winter.

The polar bear's fur is bright white. This is a perfect **camouflage** in the frontier snow and ice. They feed mainly on seals, using ice floes as a waiting platform from which to hunt. They can move very fast over the pack ice as well as being excellent swimmers. Polar bears will eat almost anything they can kill. Huge and powerfully built, they can weigh 770 kilograms (kg) (1,700 pounds [lbs]). They are very aggressive and can easily outrun a human.

Climate change is the biggest threat to polar bears. The ice platforms that polar bears use when hunting are melting. As this happens, they are less able to find food, and recent studies show that the average size of polar bears is falling. If the ice continues to disappear, many polar bears may die of starvation or drown.

▲ *Polar bears rifling through rubbish dumps and bins has been a problem in villages and towns in northern Canada in recent years. Experts believe the bears are being forced from their icy hunting grounds in search of food.*

In their own words ...

Dave Hill was forced to abandon a **solo, unsupported trek** from Canada to the North Pole. The Scotsman then faced a life or death challenge of finding an ice runway strong enough to allow a rescue plane to land. Before being rescued, he had a close encounter with a polar bear, but he said:

❝ Polar bears are the least of my problems right now – I am far more worried about thinning ice. I have made a mental note to brush up on what's going on with global warming when I get back home. ❞

SEA HUNTERS

Two of the deadliest sea creatures are found in the polar regions, the orca and the leopard seal. In the past, these fearsome **predators** have been heavily hunted by humans for food. They must now survive new threats posed by humans.

KILLER WHALE

The orca is the world's largest, toughest dolphin. Great strength, speed, and one of the biggest brains in the animal kingdom make the species a supreme polar predator. The more common name, killer whale, comes from the animal's habit of attacking whales. A boy was charged while swimming in a bay in Alaska, but there have been no other orca attacks on humans on the frozen frontier.

Humans, however, are a threat to the orca. The 1989 **Exxon Valdez oil spill** had deadly effects on orcas in Alaska. One **pod**, or group, was caught in the spill and about half of those had disappeared by the following year. The spill also reduced the amount of local **prey** species, such as salmon, so there was less food for the orcas, further reducing their numbers in the region.

▲ *Orcas are not whales, as many people think, but are in fact dolphins. They are the fastest mammals in the sea.*

SURVIVAL OF THE SPECIES

Like other animals at the top of the **food chain**, the orca is under threat from certain chemicals produced by industrial processes. These **pollutants** are carried to polar seas by ocean currents and at high levels can be poisonous to sea life. Some scientists believe that human activity, even something as harmless as whale watching, is upsetting patterns of orca behaviour.

LEOPARD OF THE SEA

Earning the name leopard seal from their patterned skin, these Antarctic seals are ferocious hunters. They prey on penguins, fish, and squid, as well as other seals. Up to 3.65 m (12 ft) in length, and weighing more than 450 kg (1,000 lbs), they have huge heads with extremely sharp front teeth. The seals shred their prey in a death shake, whipping it from side to side at lightning speed.

A member of Ernest Shackleton's team was chased by a leopard seal before it was shot dead by the ship's second-in-command. In July 2003, Kirsty Brown, a marine biologist snorkelling off the Antarctic Peninsula, was grabbed, pulled down, and drowned by a leopard seal.

ANIMAL AID

Leopard seals are helping humans to learn more about climate change. Many leopard seals can be found in one particular region of Antarctica where there are large numbers of penguins, the Antarctic Peninsula. This part of the Antarctic is one of the most rapidly warming places on Earth. Leopard seals will now eat whatever is available. By tracking the diets of the seals in this region, scientists can find out about changes in the food chain that may be caused by global warming. By studying a seal's whiskers, scientists are able to discover how feeding patterns have changed in the previous three years.

▼ The long, sleek leopard seal is an excellent swimmer. Its wide mouth helps to grasp prey such as seal pups and penguins.

POLAR EXPLORATION

Journeys to the polar frontiers have been undertaken for many reasons. The earliest explorers ventured into the vast and dangerous oceans of the south and north on voyages of discovery. Later voyagers sailed in search of the fish and whales that were noted by earlier explorers. In the early 1900s, the men who raced each other across the Antarctic were driven by personal ambition – they wanted to be the first to reach the pole. Today, men and women undertake difficult and hazardous journeys to the polar regions in search of new adventures.

EARLY ARCTIC EXPLORATION

The first people to explore the Arctic regions came from Asia and wanted to find and settle in new lands. Some of their modern descendants are the Inuit people of North America. In the late 1500s, Europeans ventured into the icy seas of the Arctic regions. They went in search of a safe route for sea trade, the **Northwest Passage**.

▼ *An early whaling boat attacks a northern right whale. Hundreds of thousands of whales were hunted in the 19th century.*

FIRST TO THE FRONTIER

Later explorers were driven perhaps by the promise of fame and personal glory. On becoming the first recorded human to reach the North Pole in 1909, American Robert E. Peary wrote, "The prize of three centuries, my dream and ambition for 23 years. *Mine* at last."

Peary was successful because he was able to adapt to life on the frontier. Unlike many previous explorers, he studied the lives of the Inuit in order to learn about survival in the polar regions. He learned to drive a dog sled, build iglus, and wore warm fur clothing to stand up to the freezing conditions. Peary was helped on his journey by teams of native frontiersmen, who often led the way.

▲ *The Arctic explorer Robert Peary aboard the* Roosevelt *in 1909, the year that he reached the North Pole.*

In their own words ...

Early explorers were overwhelmed by frontier conditions. Some imagined they saw great sea creatures, or exaggerated accounts of those which they had seen. One such creature (perhaps an oar fish) was described by a Danish voyager off the western coast of Greenland in 1734.

" [There] appeared a very terrible sea-animal, which raised itself so high above the water, that its head reached above our maintop. It had a long, sharp snout, and blew like a whale … on the lower part it was formed like a snake, and when it went under water again … it raised its tail above the water, a whole ship length from its body. "

THE SOUTH POLE

For centuries, nothing was known about the southern frontier. The stormy seas and masses of pack ice in the Southern Ocean prevented ships from exploring the area. Maps of the world marked the region as *Terra Australis Incognita*, or "unknown southern land".

The French explorer Bouvet de Lozier (1705–86) described the difficulties that early explorers faced in the Southern Ocean. Sailing through southern seas in the 1730s, he wrote, "I saw sailors crying with cold as they hauled in the sounding line". He also described the dangers of sailing in these waters, particularly icebergs: "In effect [they] are floating rocks … If we hit one we will be lost."

▼ *The polar exploration ship* Aurora. *It was used on Antarctic voyages by Mawson and Shackleton.*

It was not until 1820 that sailors first saw Antarctica, and explorers did not set foot on the continent until 1895, when a Norwegian whaling crew went ashore.

THE RACE TO THE POLE

The race to the South Pole between British explorer Robert Falcon Scott (1868–1912) and Roald Amundsen of Norway (1872–1928) is a lesson on adapting to life on the frontier. These men led expeditions to the South Pole that both set off in late 1911.

POLAR EXPLORATION

1570s: Martin Frobisher sails into Arctic regions searching for the Northwest Passage.

1773: James Cook crosses the Antarctic Circle in search of Antarctica.

1820: Antarctica is seen for the first time in recorded history.

1839–43: James Ross is the first to go beyond the pack ice surrounding Antarctica.

1845: Sir John Franklin's expedition disappears while searching for a sea route around northern North America.

1854: Robert McClure completes the Northwest Passage.

1901–02: Robert Scott leads the first inland exploration of Antarctica.

1909: Robert Peary reaches the North Pole.

1911: Roald Amundsen reaches the South Pole.

1911–14: Douglas Mawson leads the Australasian Antarctic Expedition.

1914–16: Ernest Shackleton's team journeys to Antarctica on the *Endurance*.

1928: The first journey to Antarctica by air.

1957–58: Vivian Fuchs leads the first crossing of Antarctica.

2001: Ann Bancroft and Liv Arnesen complete the first crossing of Antarctica by women explorers.

Amundsen, like Robert Peary, studied Inuit life in the northern polar regions. He believed that many of their survival techniques could be used on the southern frontier. Amundsen used dog sleds to haul supplies. His team travelled quickly across the ice on skis. Amundsen was careful to set up supply dumps on the way to the pole, ensuring that there would be no shortages during the return journey.

Scott planned to use ponies to carry supplies at the start of his journey. These were not ideal haulage animals for polar conditions. After using the ponies for part of their journey, Scott and his team hauled supplies themselves.

TRIUMPH AND DISASTER

Amundsen reached the pole on 14 December 1911, and safely returned to base camp. Scott's men, however, struggled to drag their sleds in worsening weather. In the end, the frontier conditions proved too much for Scott's team to endure. Weak and cold after a march of 79 days, they finally reached the pole in January 1912. Their spirits sank when they found the Norwegian flag flying above Amundsen's empty tent. All five members of Scott's team died on their return journey.

◄ *Captain Robert Falcon Scott (left) and his team arrive at the South Pole to find Amundsen's tent. The Norwegian explorer's record showed that he had reached the pole weeks earlier.*

PEOPLE ON THE FRONTIER

Today about two million people live on the northern frozen frontier of the Arctic Circle in large settled towns. Industries such as logging, fishing, and mining have brought work to these areas. Other frontier people of the north live in smaller, more remote settlements.

The only permanent human settlements in Antarctica are the research stations, where a few thousand scientists live and work for extended periods of time. Both polar regions are now extremely popular destinations for tourists to visit the strange and beautiful landscapes and wildlife, or those who enjoy extreme sports.

FRONTIER SETTLEMENT

In many respects, life in a frontier town such as Igloolik in Nanavut, northern Canada, is not all that different from elsewhere. People attend school or go to work, and live in homes with telephones and Internet access, and all the latest home-entertainment systems. Libraries, supermarkets with fresh and frozen food, and ice-hockey games are all features of modern life for those who live in settled areas. It is cold but people are more likely to wear modern, down-filled jackets than the sealskin **parkas** of their ancestors.

▼ *The Arctic frontier town of Umanak in Greenland is a fishing and hunting base with a population of fewer than 1,500 people. Children in Greenland believe that Santa Claus lives near here.*

▲ *Inuit children playing street hockey in Igloolik, Nanavut, in Canada.*

HUNTING LIFE

Hunting is still an important part of life in the northern frontier. Seal and walrus hunters are more likely to travel in a motorized snowmobile than a dog sled, and many prefer to use guns rather than the **harpoons** of old. During trips to wild and remote frozen places, satellite phones will keep them in touch with their families.

RESPECTING TRADITIONS

Many native people have adopted new technologies, but continue to respect the old ways. Some still hunt walrus in the traditional manner. They drive sleds across the ice highway. They rest in basic wooden huts that are built in the villages and towed by dogs to the hunting grounds. Each hunter trains his own pack of huskies and these people judge each other by the strength and obedience of their dogs.

Some hunters continue to wear the clothing that has helped people to survive the Earth's coldest weather for centuries – polar-bear trousers, sealskin boots, and fur parkas, thinking it is better than modern clothing. "We're not opposed to new things," says one Greenland hunter. "If we found something better, we'd use it."

The native hunters who continue the old ways face new challenges. The ice sheet that covers parts of Greenland is disappearing in some places. Without platforms of drifting sea ice, seals and walrus cannot rest, eat, and give birth to pups, and hunters are unable to travel in search of food.

In their own words ...

A Greenland hunter looks out to an area of open sea. The area used to be an ice edge containing walrus, but climate change has melted the ice.

"In my whole life, and that of my father and grandfather, there has never been anything like this at this time of year. Without ice, we can't live. Without ice, we're nothing at all. "

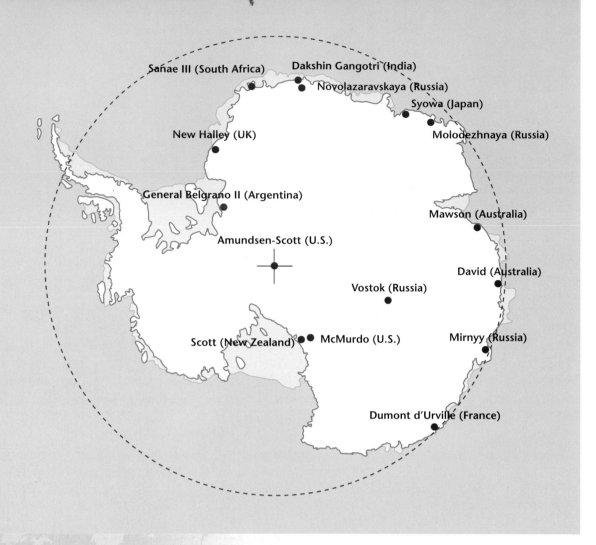

Sañae III (South Africa)
Dakshin Gangotri (India)
Novolazaravskaya (Russia)
Syowa (Japan)
New Halley (UK)
Molodezhnaya (Russia)
General Belgrano II (Argentina)
Mawson (Australia)
Amundsen-Scott (U.S.)
David (Australia)
Vostok (Russia)
Scott (New Zealand)
McMurdo (U.S.)
Mirnyy (Russia)
Dumont d'Urville (France)

▲ *Many of the research stations are on the rocky coast of Antarctica. Notice that some of the stations are named after famous polar explorers, for example Mawson and Amundsen-Scott.*

WORKING ON THE FRONTIER

According to the Royal Geographical Society, "exploration is no longer a matter of just filling in the blanks on the map, but of discovering how the Earth functions". The scientists who spend months carrying out studies at research stations in the Antarctic are helping us to learn more about the world. Climate change has made frontier research more important than ever.

There are more than 50 scientific bases in the Antarctic. The largest of these is the U.S. station McMurdo, which has grown in size to a large town, with many research laboratories, workshops, and living areas. Scientists from nearly 30 countries live and work at the Antarctic stations for many months at a time, and some stay there all year round.

DINOSAUR DISCOVERY!

Working in some of the planet's harshest conditions, fossil hunters have found two new species of dinosaur in Antarctica. This increases to eight the number of dinosaur species found on the permanently frozen southern landmass. The discovery of new species of theropod and sauropod was revealed by the National Science Foundation, the body that organizes U.S. research in Antarctica.

From *National Geographic News*, 9 March 2004

RESEARCH PIONEERS

Some of the scientific research involves drilling down through layers of ice to remove samples that were formed thousands of years ago. The samples can be studied, for example to find out about the level of pollutants when the ice was formed. So far, the atmosphere in Antarctica contains few pollutants, so the sky is very clear, and it is a great place to look at stars and **meteors**. Scientists also study weather patterns, rocks, soil, and polar plants and animals.

The important work that they do and the possibility of new discoveries help the scientists to cope with the difficulties of life on the frontier. This is just as well, because they sometimes work in the harshest frontier conditions. Much of their work is outside, and the scientists have to learn survival skills, for example abseiling into a deep crevasse, that will prepare them for an emergency situation.

FRONTIER CHALLENGES

Those who work at the stations must also cope with life in a remote part of the world, where they will be separated from family and friends for long periods of time. Loneliness and long winters, in which they rarely see the sunshine, can be gloomy. This provides a challenge for these modern-day frontiersmen and women.

The difficulties of working on a station are overcome by teamwork. The larger stations are set up to make life as comfortable as possible, with gyms and recreation rooms, in which films may be shown during winter evenings. These all help to create a strong sense of community on the frontier.

▼ *A protective dome covered in frost and ice at the Amundsen-Scott Station, the U.S. research facility in Antarctica. The dome covers buildings containing everything the scientists need to live and work. It also provides extra protection from the cold.*

VISITING THE FRONTIER

The frozen frontier has a growing number of visitors. Some make difficult journeys to remote parts of the polar regions, experiencing the harsh conditions and dangers that continue to challenge humans. Others come as tourists, enjoying the spectacular polar land- and seascapes from the comfortable surroundings of cruise ships or sightseeing planes.

▲ *The passengers on Antarctic cruises face none of the hardships of earlier polar explorers.*

MODERN ADVENTURERS

Journeys of exploration and discovery are largely a thing of the past. In the most challenging journeys to the polar regions, modern-day explorers are attempting to push personal frontiers rather than going on voyages of discovery. They are trying to set new limits of physical endurance and achievement. The adventurers who visit the polar regions are often attempting to create new records, for example the quickest solo, unsupported trek across the Antarctic. Their adventure stories satisfy the continuing human interest in great journeys.

Documentary filmmakers, particularly camera operators, also experience the very harshest frontier conditions. Those who worked on the 2006 BBC production *Planet Earth* captured dramatic new film of emperor penguins. In the "extras" scenes, they were shown working in ferocious winds as they filmed the penguins. The film also showed the very real danger posed by hungry polar bears to those who spend many days on the ice!

WHO'S WHO

Ranulph Fiennes

Sir Ranulph Fiennes is a modern-day adventurer who continues to brave the ultimate challenges of the frozen frontier. In 2000, he attempted a solo, unsupported trek to the North Pole. After his sleds fell through weak ice, Fiennes pulled them out by hand. He suffered severe frostbite to the tips of several fingers, and was forced to abandon the journey. After his return home, he is supposed to have attempted to remove the fingers himself with a saw!

THRILL SEEKERS

A small number of visitors travel to Antarctica in search of extreme conditions for adventure sports. Sky diving, climbing, surfing, diving, and ski walking are no longer uncommon in the polar regions. Increasing numbers of people are flying into ice airfields to climb mountains or ski to the South Pole. Ensuring the safety of these visitors may become a problem in the future.

POLAR TOURISM

Some people visit polar lands, usually the Arctic, to experience the lifestyle of its native inhabitants. They go ice-hole fishing, ride on dog sleds, and learn how to build an iglu. It's a relatively safe frontier experience, since the visitors are usually looked after by Inuit guides. Local people are paid for the many services to visitors. The money that these lifestyle tourists bring helps to support towns and communities in the Arctic regions.

Cruise ships, in which visitors are transported from place to place on fully supplied luxury boats, now regularly visit the polar regions. These visitors can view icebergs and other dramatic frozen features in safety and snug comfort. Some people now take flights over Antarctica from Australia or South America.

▼ *A wildlife photographer gets close to a walrus at Baffin Island, northern Canada. The extreme conditions in which polar creatures live draws professional photographers and film crews to these remote regions.*

FRONTIER SPOILS

Both the Southern Ocean and the Arctic Ocean contain large quantities of fish and whales. Beneath the surface of the frozen frontier, particularly the lands that border the Arctic Ocean, lie rich quantities of oil, coal, and natural gas. Humans continue to **exploit** these **resources**, venturing to the frontier for the purpose of transporting them to settled lands for **profit**. This has affected the frontier **environment** – the landscape, wildlife, and native people of the polar regions.

▼ An Antarctic fur seal rests in a field of rusted barrels, the remains of an abandoned whaling station.

WHALING AND FISHING

During the 18th and 19th centuries, large fleets of ships sailed to the northern and southern frontiers in search of whales. Some species were hunted to the point of **extinction**. More recently, over-fishing, where fish are removed from the sea in such large numbers that it is impossible for them to recover by breeding, has changed the environment of the polar seas.

GRABBING THE LAND

The profit-making activities of humans have also changed the polar landscape. Logging, although providing jobs for some local people, has contributed to the removal of vast forests in the taiga on the sub-Arctic. Rigs in the far northern regions extract gas and oil from beneath the ice. This is transported south along vast pipelines, the biggest of which run through Alaska in the United States and Siberia in Russia.

Leaks in oil pipelines have polluted large areas of land. At sea, oil spills from tankers – such as the *Exxon Valdez* – that are used to transport oil to southern lands have created vast slicks, threatening all forms of wildlife.

SETTING LIMITS?

The frozen regions are special environments that have built up over hundreds of thousands of years. Human activity that changes the frontier could upset the balance of **ecosystems** to such an extent that they would not recover. But businesses continue to eye-up the Arctic for new ways to exploit frontier oil, minerals, and other resources.

The Antarctic faces fewer challenges from human activity. It is a long way from settled regions, and the severe conditions make mining and drilling difficult and expensive. More importantly, the Antarctic Treaty (see pages 40–41) attempts to preserve the wilderness, and mining is banned until 2048.

FUTURE IMPACT

Scientists are careful to avoid damaging the environment during their work, but some of the research stations are now the size of large towns. The United States has built a 1,600-km (1,000-mile) road between its coastal base and the South Pole.

Organizations like the World Wildlife Fund (WWF) remind polar tourists of the need to protect the wilderness, particularly by minimizing waste and pollution. However, as more and more humans travel to the frontier, some of the features of the frozen wilderness, particularly its remote and wild beauty, may slowly change.

▶ One of 16 offshore oil-drilling platforms in the Cook Inlet, Alaska, which contains large oil and gas deposits.

EMPTYING THE SEAS

Fish, squid, and thousands of tonnes of **krill** are taken from the Southern Ocean each year on large factory ships. The fish is processed and frozen while it is still at sea, and ships do not return to port until they are full. Some scientists predict that many species of fish will disappear by 2050 as a result of over-fishing.

PROTECTING THE FRONTIER

There are a number of ways in which the frozen frontiers are protected and the speed of change in polar environments is managed. In the Arctic regions, wildlife parks have been set up to protect environments from further human interference. Areas of land have also been created in which native people are able to live and to make choices about the way their lands are developed.

THE ANTARCTIC TREATY

The Antarctic Treaty was created in 1961. It protects the frozen wilderness from the damage caused by wars or nuclear testing, and bans the removal of resources for profit. It defines the Antarctic as a natural reserve, devoted to scientific research. The Antarctic Treaty has banned mining until 2048. More than 40 countries have now joined the agreement. This represents 80 percent of the world's people.

▲ Protesters of the environmental organization Greenpeace at a meeting of the International Whaling Commission (IWC). After a long period of decline, the hunting of whales is returning.

In their own words ...

An Antarctic Survey team member describes how the southern frozen frontiers might be protected.

"At the southern end of our world, those who share the challenges of distance and cold to visit the ice-bound continent have developed a tradition of warm co-operation. Such co-operation ... is cemented by the Antarctic Treaty."

THE CHALLENGES AHEAD

So far, the treaty has worked well and has encouraged scientists from around the world to work together. However, if large quantities of valuable resources such as oil and gas are found, pressure to allow drilling will increase. Some campaigners believe that there is a growing attempt by some countries to grab land in the Antarctic. This is so they will be ready to mine the resources that lie under the ice cap if the treaty ends.

Humans have now left footprints across many parts of the frozen frontier. Many people believe that the key to protecting the frontier is human activity that is **sustainable**. It is necessary for humans to exploit some of the Earth's resources. But this needs to be done in a way that does not damage the environment, by removing resources so that they disappear permanently from the special ecosystems of the frozen regions.

There are many examples of careless human behaviour in the polar regions, but there are also reasons to be positive. Throughout history, explorers have learned survival skills from native people. Scientists from many different countries share knowledge and discoveries in the Antarctic. The Antarctic Treaty is a good attempt to encourage co-operation among humans in the interests of understanding life on the frozen frontier, and the rest of the planet.

▼ *A passenger on one of the Quark Expedition voyages. Aboard each ship is a staff of expedition leaders, naturalists, and lecturers. The voyages are organized in a way that minimizes impact or disturbances to wildlife.*

FACTS AND STATISTICS

FRONTIER FICTION

The Ancient Greeks believed that the polar regions were warm and fertile!

ALL ABOUT ANTARCTICA

- Total land mass about 14.2 million square km (5.5 million square miles).
- Covered by an ice cap with an average thickness of 2 km (1.2 miles).

COLDEST ON EARTH

- Coldest average temperature – Plateau Station, Antarctica, with an average of –56.6°C (–69.8°F).
- Lowest temperature ever – Vostock Station, Antarctica. On 21 July 1983, it dropped to –89.2°C (–128.6°F).
- Temperatures in Antarctica are 10–30° colder than at similar latitudes in the northern hemisphere.

DEEP FREEZE

In the coldest Antarctic temperatures, human flesh freezes in seconds and breathing the air can cause lung damage.

ALL ABOUT ICE

- About 70 percent of the Arctic Ocean is covered by ice throughout the year.

Quantity of ice in Antarctica:

- 2.5 million square km (1 million square miles) in summer.
- 20.5 million square km (8 million square miles) in winter.
- The thickness of ice at the South Pole is 2,800 m (9,186 ft).
- At height of summer, only 2 percent of the Antarctic continent is free of ice; most of this is in the Antarctic Peninsula.

ALL ABOUT ICEBERGS

- Icebergs are made of fresh water, not sea water.
- 80–90 percent of an iceberg is under water.
- The biggest icebergs can tower 150 m (492 ft) above water.

SUN, SUN, SUN

The cold in Antarctica can create optical illusions. The air holds millions of tiny ice crystals and these create a huge wheel of light with an "extra" sun on each side. These are called **parhelions**.

SUPER STINGER

The lion's mane jellyfish is a species that lives in cold water and is found in some Arctic seas. It causes painful, potentially deadly stings. The largest are 2.5 m (8 ft) wide, with tentacles that can trail for more than 30 m (98 ft).

MASSIVE WHALES

The largest whale of the Southern Ocean is the blue whale, which grows up to 30 m (98 ft) in length and can weigh as much as 150 tonnes (165 tons). A fully grown blue whale eats about 40 million krill per day during the feeding season.

BIG BRUTES

Elephant seals can weigh up to 4 tonnes (4.4 tons) and measure 7 m (23 ft) in length. The male Atlantic walrus can grow to almost 4 m (13 ft) long and weighs as much as 1,400 kg (3,086 lbs). Its tusks can reach 1 m (3 ft) in length.

SMALL FRY

The smallest land animal in Antarctica is an insect less than 1.3 cm (0.5 in) in length. It is a wingless **midge** that lives near penguin colonies.

SNOW GOGGLES

Polar bears have an extra eyelid that helps protect their eyes from the glare of the sun from the ice cap.

TOOTHLESS BEAST

Weddell seals survive closer to the South Pole than any other mammals. They live under the ice, cutting breathing holes through the surface. This wears out their teeth and some seals die of starvation as they become unable to hunt and catch prey.

ANTI-FREEZE ADAPTATION

Some Antarctic fish have anti-freeze in their bodies. This allows their body fluids to remain liquid at temperatures below 0°C (32°F), the point at which ice forms.

SUPER SCIENCE STATIONS

Many of the Antarctic research stations are built on rock on the coast. The U.S. Amundsen-Scott base at the South Pole is built on slowly shifting ice.

INUIT HOMELAND

- Nanavut is the name of the region of northern Canada that is a homeland for Inuit people.
- It covers almost 2 million square km (0.8 million square miles) and is about one-fifth of Canada's land mass.
- Nanavut means "our land" in Inuit language.

TOUGH TUSKS

Walruses use their tusks to haul themselves on to Arctic ice floes and smash breathing holes in the ice.

ALL ABOUT GLOBAL WARMING

- Arctic sea ice has thinned by about 40 percent in the past 30 years and it has shrunk by as much as 10–15 percent.
- The average temperature in the Antarctic Peninsula has risen 2.5°C since 1940. This is about 10 times as fast as global warming elsewhere.

LEFT IN THE COLD

The United States and Russia built defences that stretched from Alaska to Greenland. Most of these military bases and spy listening posts, together with the odd spy plane, are now abandoned.

FURTHER RESOURCES

BOOKS

Arctic and Antarctic, Barbara Taylor, Geoff Brightling (photographer), DK Eyewitness Guides, 2000

Extreme Survival – Polar Regions, Sally Morgan, Chrysalis, 2003

Polar Regions, Paul Mason, Hodder Wayland, 2004

Saving Our World: Polar Regions, Jen Green, Franklin Watts, 2003

True Polar Adventure Stories, Paul Dowsell, Usborne Publishing Ltd, 2002

WEBSITES

www.aad.gov.au
The site of the Australian Antarctic Expedition. This site contains lots of facts about the southern polar regions. There are lots of FAQs from schools to which station residents have responded.

www.antarctica.ac.uk
The site of the British Antarctic Survey. The Schools Zone and Guided Tour sections are especially good. This site also features diary entries by those who live and work at the Antarctic stations, and it is possible to send an email to one of the scientists.

www.spri.cam.ac.uk
The website of the Scott Polar Research Institute in Cambridge, UK. This site contains a great online resource for researchers and historians, particularly the Virtual Shackleton section, which has many original letters and diary entries by one of the most famous polar explorers.

www.panda.org
The website of the World Wildlife Fund, this contains lots of information about polar geography and conservation issues.

www.south-pole.com
A massive website devoted to polar exploration. This contains detailed biographies of all the most famous polar explorers, and some brilliant pictures of ships and maps.

www.nationalgeographic.com
The website of the *National Geographic* magazine has plenty of information on the Arctic and Antarctic regions. Check out Life in the Deep Freeze for wildlife and Research in Polar Seas for the latest technology.

www.yourexpedition.com
This site tells the story of explorers Ann Bancroft and Liv Arnesen's historic trek across the Antarctic in 2001, the first by women. Be inspired by them to undertake your own journey!

www.mnh.si.edu/arctic
The website for the Smithsonian Institution's Arctic Studies Center, which focuses on the lives and history of people of the northern polar regions.

www.usap.gov
The website of the United States Antarctic Program, with loads of information and photographs of the regions and the research going on there.

FILMS

Planet Earth – Ice Worlds and From Pole to Pole
BBC, 2006
Attenborough's team returns to the polar regions with the latest camera equipment. The film features stunning footage of male emperor penguins incubating eggs during the freezing mid-winter months. The extras section reveals the superhuman efforts of the camera teams that brave polar storms and hungry polar bears to get these shots!

Eyewitness Interactive – Arctic & Antarctic
Freemantle, 2000
Choose your entry point and explore the North and South Poles in 14 extreme chapters of BBC and DK film as well as state-of-the-art computer graphics.

The March of the Penguins
Warner Bros., 2005
This award-winning documentary film follows the journey of emperor penguins as they travel hundreds of kilometres across Antarctica, in freezing cold temperatures, icy winds, and through deep, treacherous waters.

GLOSSARY

adapt physical development or behaviour that helps plants and animals to survive

camouflage adaptation that allows a species to blend in with its surroundings, making it difficult to spot

caribou large reindeer

continent mass of land. There are seven continents on Earth – Africa, Asia, Australia, North America, South America, Europe, and Antarctica.

crevasse deep crack in a glacier or snowfield

ecosystem way in which plants, animals, and other organisms live together in a local environment

environment all living and non-living things that occur naturally on Earth; the Earth's natural surroundings

exploit to remove natural resources, for example food, timber, or minerals, from the environment

extinction when an animal or plant has been hunted or used to the point where it no longer exists

Exxon Valdez oil spill tanker that spilled up to 30 million gallons of oil in Prince William Sound, Alaska. As a result, thousands of animals died in the following months.

food chain group of living things that depend on one another for food, by eating each other. For example, plankton are eaten by fish, which are in turn eaten by seals; seals are eaten by orca.

frostbite damage to parts of the body caused by exposure to extreme cold

glacier permanent sheet of ice formed from compressed ice and snow crystals

greenhouse gase gas such as carbon dioxide in the Earth's atmosphere that causes global warming

harpoon spear-like object used for hunting. Traditional Inuit harpoons are made of carved whalebone.

hypothermia condition in which the human body temperature drops below the level required for essential bodily functions to take place

iceberg chunk of ice that breaks off a glacier and floats out to sea

ice floes floating chunks of ice that are formed as pack ice melts

iglu temporary shelter made from blocks of snow or ice

inhospitable wild and without shelter

kayak Inuit canoe made of a wooden frame covered with waterproof animal skins

krill tiny shrimp-like animals that live in the sea

lichen type of plant formed by a combination of algae and fungus that is usually found on bare rock and trees

mammal animal that is warm-blooded, breathes air, and suckles its young – for example humans, whales, and seals

meteors rocks that have entered the Earth's atmosphere from elsewhere in space

midge tiny, two-winged fly, similar to a mosquito

midnight sun permanent sunlight during the polar summer

migrate annual movement of birds or animals from one part of the world to another

mineral substance found in the Earth, which can be mined – for example gold and iron

navigation using maps and charts to plan the course of a journey

Northwest Passage route from Europe to Asia across or around northern North America

pack ice solid ice that forms when the sea freezes over large areas

pancake ice ice that forms at the sea's surface, in less calm conditions than pack ice

parhelion bright spot that sometimes appears on either side of the sun, like a luminous ring or halo

parka heavy, fur jacket with a hood. Traditional Inuit parkas are treated with oil to keep them waterproof.

pioneer person who travels to wilderness areas, preparing the way for others to follow

pod group of whales or other sea mammals such as orca

polar night permanent darkness during the polar winter

pollutant substance that makes something dirty or impure, especially waste from human activity

predator animal that hunts other animals for food

prey living thing that is caught and eaten by another animal or bird

profit money made from a business activity

prospector someone who visits a region in search of valuable resources such as gold

research station settlement that is designed for humans to carry out scientific studies

resources anything that can be used to human advantage. Natural resources include oil and minerals.

skidoo vehicle for moving across snow, with tracks and a ski at the front for steering

sled vehicle for travelling across snow and ice. Traditional Inuit sleds are pulled by a team of up to 15 husky dogs.

solo, unsupported trek journey made by one man or woman without the help of a supply team

sustainable human activity that attempts to provide the best outcome for the human and natural environments, now and for the future

taiga southern edge of the northern polar region, beyond the tundra. Dense forests cover this area.

tundra flat, treeless lands between the Arctic ice sheet and the taiga, the forested edge of the Arctic region

wilderness unsettled and wild area of land that is in its natural state

windchill cooling effect of a strong wind when it takes away heat from the body

INDEX